GATHERING THE FRAGMENTS

Dedicated

To the People of St. Agnes Parish,
the mustard seed of our diocese;
for their faith, hope and love
1978-1987

and

To Sr. Marcella Clancy, SSJ,
in celebration of her 25th anniversary,
September 1, 1986

and

To Sr. Susan Dinnin, SP,
in celebration of her 25th anniversary,
September 18, 1987
my friends and co-workers at St. Agnes
for so many years.

With gratitude to Nan Merrill
for her manuscript work and typing.

Gathering
—the—
Fragments

A Gospel Mosaic

REV. EDWARD J. FARRELL

ALBA·HOUSE   NEW·YORK

SOCIETY OF ST. PAUL, 2187 VICTORY BLVD., STATEN ISLAND, NEW YORK 10314

ST PAULS

Acknowledgments

Excerpts from THE JERUSALEM BIBLE, copyright © 1966 by Darton, Longman & Todd, Ltd. and Doubleday & Company, Inc. Used by permission of the publisher.

Excerpts from the English translation of The Roman Missal © 1973, International Committee on English in the Liturgy, Inc. All rights reserved.

Original hard bound edition © 1987 by Ave Maria Press
All rights reserved.

Library of Congress Cataloging-in-Publication Data

Farrell, Edward J., Rev.
    Gathering the fragments: a gospel mosaic / Edward J. Farrell.
        p.   cm.
    Originally published: Notre Dame, Ind.: Ave Maria Press, © 1987.
    Original Library of Congress Card Number: 87-70902
    ISBN 0-8189-0860-2
    1. Meditations.   I. Title.
BX2182.2.F37   1999
242 — dc21   99-12718
                                                       CIP

Produced and designed in the United States of America by the
Fathers and Brothers of the Society of St. Paul,
2187 Victory Boulevard, Staten Island, New York 10314-6603,
as part of their communications apostolate.

ISBN: 0-8189-0860-2

Printing Information:

Current Printing - first digit   1   2   3   4   5   6   7   8   9   10

Year of Current Printing - first year shown

1999   2000   2001   2002   2003   2004   2005   2006

Table of Contents

An Opening Note

The Spirit too comes to help us in our weakness.
For when we cannot choose words in order to
pray properly, the Spirit himself expresses our plea
in a way that could never be put into words.

Romans 8:26

The way to get into my book is to expect nothing.
It was written that way. At a glance it will seem
like nothing, a poor book. But if you feel poor in
spirit, if you are really looking for the Spirit, then
the Spirit will surprise you by drawing something
out of the nothingness of my writing.

I am always surprised when someone quotes
my own words back to me. I realize those words
did not come from me alone. They tell me much
about the spirit of the person who finds and quotes
them. The Spirit speaks through my words, which
have come from something in my spirit, to the
spirit and soul in another. And hearing that person speak those words back to me communicates
something of the spirit that received them. What

a beautiful and holy experience — to have the spirit in another confirm the Spirit within.

Whenever I write, I must wrestle with my demon. I must overcome a great resistance and hesitancy within. Like Mailer, I recognize that "you have to care about people to share your perception with them, especially if it is a perception which can give them life." Out of my poorness, my nothingness, I care enough to want the Spirit which dwells in me to meet, and, if the time is right, to activate the Spirit abiding within you.

Diary of a City Priest

> To follow Him means to take the downward path
> to poverty and littleness by living and sharing with
> the poor, by living with our own poverty and there
> to discover the source of life flowing forth from
> His Presence.
>
> Jean Vanier

I am waiting for God, yet I feel he is already here.
My day gets filled, at times without my decision,
and what I intended to do gets stacked higher and
higher on the pile of things to be done. But Jesus
does not pass me by. He touches me in a thousand
different ways.

I am often waiting for people who are not yet
here. I am an urban priest, the pastor of an inner-
city parish. Sometimes I think I am running a
"Good Samaritan Inn" on the road from Jerusalem to Jericho. And I am haunted by the endless
parade of people marching by, disappearing into
the receding distance, the pilgrims of the transcendent, of "the way, the truth and the life."

I am haunted too by the innocent bystanders, the observers of the river of life and the river of belief. This is our journey of faith. Some jump in and swim, some follow it to the sea. Others just come and look, then back away from the edge.

Everyone is on the Emmaus journey. Sooner or later Jesus catches up with us and walks and talks with us as we go our way. Something usually prevents us from recognizing him, but wherever we are and wherever we go, he is with us even though we cannot name why our hearts are smoldering within.

Faith is a spark, God is the fire. The faith of a Christian today is personal and humble. Faith is always a beginning, a pilgrimage. Jesus is always ahead of us, and we are so often hesitant, if not reluctant, disciples.

We are fragile, earthen vessels, so easily shattered. In my weakness is God's strength, in my wounds he reveals himself. It is not so much my faith as God's faithfulness. Maturing faith is attention to this living presence of God in the depths of one's being as one is drawn into Jesus' life of action for justice.

Each one of us is but a fragment of Jesus, one member of the body, one branch, one leaf of the vine. Only together can we grasp the whole. We need each other to discover the whole Christ, the whole person each of us is called to be.

When we have been touched by Jesus, when the Spirit is stirred up in the depths of our being, when we dare to own Paul's words, "I live now not I, but Christ lives in me," then we can no longer live for ourselves alone. I am compelled to share my faith with others. God's presence in me overflows into the lives of others and I become receptive to his presence and power in others. You are different from me but we were born involved in each other.

Contemplation is like holding a magnifying glass to God long enough for him to burn his imprint upon you so that you never can forget his presence in your life, so that you become a burning bush. Contemplation is looking so deeply into things and people that you are continually being ignited by the rays and hidden flames emanating from the splendor of God's presence in all creation.

Everything that exists has its own language of inspiration and faith and praise. Teilhard de Chardin, in his *Hymn of the Universe*, speaks of "the intense personal experience of God's goodness in providing for us and placing us in so magnificent and friendly a setting." Chardin's faith was inspired by his inability to contain his sense of wonder.

The beauty of the world remains an ever present consolation and illumination. Miracles of beauty continually manifest God's presence:

- I am awakened by the full moon suspended in benediction over the sleeping city.
- I am lifted out of bed by the dancing of the sun on the shimmering leaves of the early morning breeze outside the window.
- I am humbled by the silence and wonder of a gentle four-year-old, who joins in prayer for

half an hour before school opens.

- I am sustained in faith by the young man with a kidney transplant and an amputated leg, who affixes his crucifix to the hospital wall as a sign of the One who is with him.
- I am inspired by the family who adopts their fourth handicapped child in gratitude for all that the Lord has given them.
- I am taught by the woman dying of cancer: "Don't hurry… don't talk."
- I am in wonder at the senile person who returns to full clarity and joins in all the prayers in the presence of the Eucharist.

I sense what I call the loving companion presence through each person in my day. When I allow God to lift all things up with a joyful heart, I know the weaving of that presence among the prayer, work, frustrations and laughter of the day; yet I must say that he is my great unknown, the immense secret that I carry within myself, a secret even from me, that always remains secret.

How patiently God has waited for me to discover this presence within myself! How difficult to be patient as I wait for others to experience this secret within their own hearts! The fragments gathered here are reflections — however veiled — of God's presence as experienced by a city parish priest who is praying for patience and desiring most to offer Eucharist, to live Eucharist, to help others become Eucharist in this broken world.

The Gift of Reverence

Then he said, "I tell you solemnly, unless you change and become like little children you will never enter the kingdom of heaven."

Matthew 18:3

What is it to experience reverence? Have you been carried away by God? Have you had a moment of rapture, of ecstasy? Have you ever been carried away by nature? Have you ever experienced a feeling of deep reverence toward yourself? Have you ever been melted by the reverence and love of another person?

Reverence is the natural virtue of the child. A child is always filled with reverence. Everything is so totally new, so fresh; the child is ever surprised. Try to remember the last time you saw something you had never seen before. In a real sense, this is our experience in every moment — everything is new. We so often fail to look — really look — at one another. Each day we all wear a new face, a face different from all the other days of our life. We need not only the time to look closely at our own faces or the faces of those we meet, we need the awareness of reverence that makes this deep looking a grace and blessing, a participation in God's vision.

We are all called to awaken the little child within ourselves, the child who looks at the world with wonder and excitement and an unselfconscious reverence. We need that kind of reverence. For the opposite of reverence is not simply jealousy, it is violence. Not only the blatant violence of death, disease, injustice and abuse, but the subtle forms of violence — carelessness, rejection, fear, insecurity, envy — are ways in which we fail to reverence the world around us. Perhaps the saddest kind of violence is the violence we do to ourselves. We fail to appreciate, to reverence, who we are and who it is that lives in us. And inasmuch as we violate the gift of the person God calls us to be, we deny others the reverence of affirming God within them. Jesus tells us that we must love God, and love our neighbors as ourselves. This demands that we first love ourselves and let ourselves be loved by God. Only then can we know what the genuine reverence of love is.

Reverence has something to do with holiness and wholeness. It is a word ordinarily ascribed to God alone. When we speak about reverence in regard to ourselves we speak of the holiness of our relationship with God. This wholeness, this holiness, is given to us not because we are without sin, but in spite of our sin. We have to believe that God loves us so much that even though we are sinners we are holy. And we are holy in a way that we give holiness to others. We have been loved so much that there is enough left over to give to others. Love enables us to see into the depths of other people's lives. This inner stream of God's love, like running water, always refreshes us so that we might offer a cup to others.

The mystery of God's giving is that he gives so much. Jesus gave his very life for love of the world. We are so constrained by our human limitations that we can love only with a small piece of ourselves. God cannot love except totally, completely, unconditionally. When we ask for expressions of his love, our very requests impose limits, and yet we are constantly amazed at the way he transcends those limits. We ask for a grain of sand and he gives us the beach; we ask for a drop of water and he gives us the ocean; we ask for life and he gives us eternity. God's gifts are his way of showing reverence for us; our reverence for him must come in our grateful response to these gifts.

Reverence is very closely aligned with faith. Our distinctively Catholic experience of Jesus himself in the Eucharist increases our reverence in a special way. In celebrating one Mass, we celebrate the mystery of Jesus to discover more deeply who he is. We take time to uncover what has happened to us and in us because of Jesus' presence in our life.

We discover how Jesus touches things, how he affects everything in the world, and how his presence in our lives affects the way we perceive the world. In the degree that we let him love us, then in some mysterious way, we begin to love all things as he sees them, as he experiences them, as he loves them. Life takes on an awe and splendor and reverence. We get caught up in him. This becomes a prayer of captivity, a prayer of being grasped, of being held, of being touched.

When Jesus walked this earth, he had a reverence for individuals that was truly an experience of love. And he has that same reverence for us as individuals today. In some way, the radiant glory of another person, of all of nature, is the glory of earth. Each one of us, in some mysterious way, is the glory of God. Through prayer we have to discern the radiant glory of God in one another. Each one of us is a kind of prism, a rainbow; a light for one another.

Community is always a mystery of communion and communication. Through a genuine experience of community we discover the beauty of reverence toward one another; and this leads us to a deeper reverence toward ourselves. Discovering more fully that mystery of who we really are is crucial for our sense of reverence and mystery toward ourselves, which ultimately will be the measure of our sense of reverence and mystery toward one another.

Reverence includes all the experiences of life — intensity and withdrawal, up and down, light and dark, varieties and values, knowledge, childbirth, death, human love, revelation and desolation — all of the realities of which our human life is so filled. And this encompasses our whole approach to prayer.

We need newness and wonder outside of us to help to discover this universe within. We need to look at things closely, to look into the depths of another. Christ looking upon the lilies of the field made them sacramental. He looked on them with his love, and by his glance alone he clothed them with his own beauty. Though we last but a moment, like the grass of the fields that withers in a day, we take on an eternity in Christ. This is the source of the reverence and awe born in us.

Learning to Pray Again

Prayer takes a firm and steadfast hold when a small fire begins to burn in the heart.... Try not to quench this fire and it will become established in such a way that the prayer repeats itself: and then you will have within you a small murmuring stream.

The Philokalia

"I would like to pray again." What a beautiful grace to want to pray. Prayer is a gift, yet it is the work of a lifetime. Why do people stop praying? Why do they begin again? Prayer is always a lost and found phenomenon. Prayer, like each human life, has many stages of growth and development, decline and loss.

Prayer, like love, is not something one achieves once and for all. It is a special kind of consciousness, awareness, attention, presence.

Prayer is a paradox and a mystery. It can be the simplest and easiest experience of life — enjoyment of a sunset in the late summer evening, the unexpected smile of a child; or it can be the most anguishing moment of a lifetime — to say yes in the face of death or tragedy.

Prayer always remains elusive. Like a well in the desert, if you use it each day, you will always have it; if you neglect it, it disappears into the sand. Prayer springs eternal in the human heart, even though it remains underground, unfelt. As all living things turn to the sun, so all spiritual beings are drawn to God — to goodness, truth and beauty — even though many might be afraid to speak his name.

Prayer is always a surprise, something new and unexpected. The psalmist cries out, "Sing to the Lord a new song." We can never breathe an old breath, nor can we pray an old prayer. Yet the prayers that have been with us in our tradition for centuries have a way of becoming the newest and freshest prayers.

Many who temporarily let go of either church, prayer or faith have told me how they began to hear the prayers of their childhood echoing up from somewhere deep inside, and this led them to a new discovery of themselves, of God, of others. A young man told me that the most exciting experience for him in the post-Vatican II era was that he was allowed to discover his own God. This was his way of saying that he had found his own prayer, that he had discovered his own inmost self.

To pray is never to get over the wonder of being born, of being alive. To pray is to live in the profound gratitude that no matter what happens, we're ahead. More has been given than one could ever have expected. To pray is to be in reverence, in awe, in joy with some moment of each day. There are no perfect days, but there is a beautiful moment in each day that draws us into prayer, consciously or unconsciously.

Contemplation is continuous communion with Jesus — it is living in him and letting him live in us. What a gift! Perhaps this is why Jesus tells us about "the need to pray continually and never lose heart" (Lk 18:1), never become discouraged. Jesus is not speaking only to monks or cloistered nuns. Jesus is speaking to all of us today.

Most prayer goes unrecognized. The whole world prays, and prayed long before Jesus. He did not invent prayer but he transformed it to a new height, depth and intensity. He revealed the great secret and source and consolation of prayer — I am never alone! To pray is to act on that suspicion that "in him I live and move and have my being." Someone is always embracing me. Someone is loving me as I am worth being loved. Someone knows me as I am worth being known.

Christian prayer is not our effort to reach God, but a recognition of his incredible presence always with us, drawing us deeper into ourselves and into others. God became human to be with us and in us, to bring us together. Our prayer becomes Christian when we discover our hunger for him is his hunger for us.

Jesus totally revolutionized prayer. No longer is it blind human groping for what is always beyond the grasp of body, soul and spirit. But he promised that he would come to us and his Father would come to us and they would make their home in us. It would have been enough if he had only left his word with us, but his love was so immense that he could not say good-bye. And so he committed himself to live with us and be our daily food and drink.

Jesus taught us to pray, "Give us this day our daily bread." This certainly means food for our table, but we know we cannot live on bread alone. We need "soul food," the bread that comes down from heaven. The Eucharist draws us into a new depth of prayer. Jesus feeds us with his own life, with his own breath, with his own spirit. The Eucharist nurtures us with the very prayer of Christ, with his own contemplation, with his life in the Father.

The Eucharist is the ultimate prayer of the Trinity, the deepest contemplation of the Trinity. To receive Jesus is to receive the Father; for as Jesus tells Philip: "To have seen me is to have seen the Father" (Jn 14:10). And where Jesus and the Father are, there is the Holy Spirit, the mutual gift of the Father and Son to us.

The Eucharist is the most tangible expression we can have of the Trinity, but not without faith, not without contemplation. The Eucharist draws us into contemplation, to an ever deeper consciousness of the Trinity. Each Eucharist deepens and activates the indwelling presence of the Father, Son and Holy Spirit. Paul wrote to the Corinthians, "Didn't you realize that you were God's temple and that the Spirit was living in you?" (1 Cor 3:16). The energy and radiation of the Trinity within us enables us also to contemplate the Father, Son and Holy Spirit in others.

Christian prayer is always a response to a presence already felt. The awareness of a desire to pray again is already prayer. As the desert fathers so often said, "If you want to pray, you are already praying." And Paul gave the Ephesians this example of his own prayer:

> This, then is what I pray,
> kneeling before the Father;
> from whom every family,
> whether spiritual or natural,
> takes its name:
>
> Out of his infinite glory,
> may he give you the power through his
> Spirit
> for your hidden self to grow strong,
> so that Christ may live in your hearts
> through faith, and then,
> planted in love and built on love,
> you will with all the saints
> have strength to grasp the breadth

and the length, the height and the depth,
until, knowing the love of Christ,
which is beyond all knowledge,
you are filled with the utter fullness of
     God.

Glory be to him whose power;
working in us,
can do infinitely more
than we can ask or imagine;
glory be to him from generation to
     generation
in the Church and in Christ Jesus
for ever and ever. Amen.

Ephesians 3:14-21

The Prayer of Reconciliation

Here is a saying that you can rely on and nobody should doubt: that Christ Jesus came into the world to save sinners. I myself am the greatest of them; and if mercy has been shown to me, it is because Jesus Christ meant to make me the greatest evidence of his inexhaustible patience for all the other people who would later have to trust in him to come to eternal life. To the eternal King, the undying, invisible and only God, be honor and glory for ever and ever. Amen.

1 Timothy 1:15-17

Jesus gives us the sacrament of reconciliation to be one of our deepest personal joys, but so many avoid it as inhuman and depressing. They have had bad experiences in the past, bad memories of the old style confession and penance. They have come to think of it as only guilt and embarrassment and have discontinued the practice at the earliest opportunity.

Jesus does not want us to feel guilty or embarrassed about coming to him in our weakness and sin. A friend does not abandon a friend when she is in need; nor did the awareness of people's sins make Jesus want to separate himself from them. Jesus felt such solidarity with the people that he experienced their guilt, their sinfulness, as his own. He felt like a sinner and asked to be washed in the river like the others. And at his baptism, the Father made it known that in drawing close to the sinner Jesus pleased him.

"Forgive us our sins as we forgive those who sin against us, and lead us not into temptation, but deliver us from evil." This is our first prayer; our first confession, and we will never finish praying it; we will never pray it deeply enough.

People do not become mature until they are honest with themselves and honest with God. Only a mature man or woman can dare to say: I am free; I make good decisions — and bad ones; I am responsible; I stumble; I am good; I sin.

Perhaps the most disturbed and immature people are those who spend all their energy denying that they have sinned, that they need healing. Jesus knows the human heart. He knows we have sinned, he knows we need his reconciliation.

> If we say we have no sin in us,
> we are deceiving ourselves
> and refusing to admit the truth;
> but if we acknowledge our sins,
> then God who is faithful and just
> will forgive our sins

and purify us from everything that is
    wrong.
To say that we have never sinned
is to call God a liar;
and to show that his word is not in us.

1 John 1:8-10

The experience of reconciliation is intended to be an experience of Jesus' love, an experience of joy, of knowing that Jesus sees something more in us. The focus of this sacrament is not our sinfulness but Jesus' goodness and healing.

Jesus knows our torment, our weakness. Like Paul we can cry out, "The good I want to do, I do not do; and the evil I want to avoid, I find myself doing. Who will deliver me? Who will free me?" Jesus is always with us to tell us "I will!" If we could only believe this truth! If we could only accept such love!

Our sins are like the grains of sand along the shore; his love is like the ocean. To think about the sacrament of reconciliation is already to begin to experience his magnetic love. Like the prodigal son, we are stirred and dare to sing, "I will arise and go to the home of my father."

This sacrament is so hard for us, not because of our sins, but because it demands such an immense act of faith — to believe he loves me even in my sins, that he loves me when I cannot love myself, that when I can't stand myself he is still with me, loving me, believing in me, hoping in me. The sacrament of reconciliation frightens us because we are afraid of his love. Remember the haunting song of Mary Magdalene in *Jesus Christ Superstar:*

> "But, if he said he loved me,
> I'd be lost, I'd be frightened."

To deny our sin, to deny our need of healing, is to run away from love, from freedom, from responsibility. If we accept his love, if we become honest with ourselves and him, he pours his Spirit into us and invites us to become disciples, co-workers, co-healers with him. Through forgiving us and encouraging us to accept his forgiveness, he teaches us to forgive others.

The Heart of the City

"You see this city? Here God lives among men.
He will make *his home among them; they shall be
his people,* and he will be their God, his name is
*God-With-Them. He will wipe away all tears from
their eyes.*"

Revelation 21:3

Jesus was a city person; he prayed over it, wept over
it, worked in it. He loved the city crowds. He
walked there and knew the city. He celebrated the
first Eucharist in the city and there initiated his
community, the church. Jesus died at the gate of
the city. There he rose from the dead. And there
the disciples waited for the descent of the Holy
Spirit to send them forth on their mission to all
the cities of the world.

Here in Detroit, where I live, the New Center area is dominated by the International Head-
quarters of General Motors, Ford Hospital,
Wayne State University, and the Art and Medical
Centers. West Grand Boulevard is a contempo-

rary Via Dolorosa, a way of the cross that so many are compelled to walk in poverty and suffering each day of their lives. Rosa Parks Boulevard is a renaissance neighborhood, a light in the darkness, a sign of hope and promise for today and tomorrow. These are some of the features of city life in the twentieth century.

Jesus' love of the city and his compassion and concern for the multitudes gives us a vision of hope for our own lives and the lives of those around us. Jesus can be deep in the heart of our metropolitan cities. It is good to have a contemplative parish in the heart of the city to provide an oasis for the thousands of people who live and work there.

This contemplative oasis in the urban desert is anchored in a parish of ordinary and faithful people who have chosen to live in the heart of the city. Through their own experience of the hardships of city life with its alienation, its struggles, its works, its restraints, its anonymity and violence, they know the stress, the noise and pollution, the joys and sorrows, the evil and goodness of the city.

They live in solidarity with the people of the city and wish to offer them a place of welcome and hospitality, a place of deep silence alive with prayer, a place of rest and healing. The parish becomes a home where all people, whatever their social or religious background, age or outlook on life, are invited to come and share in a common search for Christ.

The early Christians went out to the natural desert to do battle with the devil, trying to find God in the struggle. Today's Christians enter into the new deserts in the midst of the city in order to fight against its illusions, its loneliness, its violence.

Here they seek out its beauty, its yearnings, its innermost values, singing a new song to the praise and glory of God. They want to be deeply rooted within the city life and they enfold the city itself within their prayer.

It makes no sense to praise the Lord of the Universe and the Lord of History and be unconcerned about Detroit, about Calcutta, about Tokyo. It makes no sense to follow the Son of Man without trying to find him in the heart of every person.

It makes no sense to live through this day without being aware that the Holy Spirit pervades every second of it. It is not a choice between contemplation of God and working for humanity. Rather, it is to bring together contemplation and action, prayer and work.

In the city, where everything is passing, God alone remains. If the city is a "mystery of iniquity," it is also a holy city. The Lord lives here and it is here that we want to contemplate him. The violence and fear in the inner city have become an environment that desperately needs contemplation. The ominous worldwide threat of nuclear terror can only be counterbalanced by a power greater than destruction.

The new sanctuary is contemplation in solidarity with the people of the city and the world. The scenarios of nuclear night and a nuclear winter compel us to hope and to search for new light, for a new spring. The human heart will submit to only so much psychic numbness. Then tremors begin to be felt in the depths, an eruption builds up and pressures forth. The spiritquake may be underground but its seismic effects circle the globe.

Summer Presence

There is a season for everything,
a time for every occupation under heaven.
Ecclesiastes 3:1

How easy it is to pray in good times, on beautiful days! This is the summer of our spirit and prayer. Often we find God's "trace elements" in the splendor and fullness of nature and people. The joy and readiness of summer lifts us constantly to the presence that fills our being.

The summertimes of our lives are times to rest and appreciate what we have, to relax and enjoy, to celebrate the extravagance and exuberance of summer, to remember, to pause, to let the joy and wonder of becoming like little children again well up within us. Summer is a time to be carefree, to laugh and play and be silly, to be a clown, to unwind, to be foolish. It is a time also to be free to do nothing, to be present in grateful receptivity, wordless awe, silent simplicity.

Every moment is God's own good time. We

have what we seek. We don't have to rush after it. It will make itself known to us. All time is free time. Every moment, every hour is a gift. We have time. It cannot be saved. And it is spent freely when we give it away.

What was Jesus' experience of summer? How did he live out those thirty summers in Nazareth? I wonder what his favorite game and pastime was? What adventures did he have with his friends from the village? What mischief did he get into?

I wonder if he ever went to Mount Carmel to the northwest of Nazareth to look upon the sun setting into the Mediterranean? Nazareth was built on a hilltop and from the cliff Jesus could easily see Mount Tabor southeast of his village. Often he must have seen the sun rise over that mountain.

Through Nazareth there ran a highway that connected Sepphoris to a secondary road joining Damascus to Egypt. What stories and adventures Jesus must have heard from merchants and visitors to his village!

And Luke tells us "every year his parents used to go to Jerusalem for the feast of Passover" (Lk 2:41). What a journey that must have been for Jesus each year! What excitement and wonder for a young boy!

He must have formed many friendships. He loved to go to dinner. He was not afraid to ask, "What do you have to eat?" or to say, "Give me a drink." Jesus welcomed everyone. Everyone was drawn to him. He felt at home with the sick, the handicapped, the poor, the abandoned. He loved little children. He had an outgoing, warm, loving personality, and yet he was a man of solitude. He would rise early in the morning and go out to a quiet place to pray. He loved to spend a night in prayer. He had a great love for nature. He knew the lilies of the field and the birds of the air. In Mark's gospel, Jesus' favorite terrain is walking along the lake; in Matthew's gospel it is the mountains; in Luke, it is the road as they walked to Jerusalem; in John, it is the City and the Temple.

How ordinary was Jesus' thirty years in Nazareth? As ordinary as your life and mine. He must have absorbed all these summers in his heart as he lived them. His Nazareth summers invite us to contemplate his waiting, his compassion, his work, his silence, his rest, his play, his secrets, his joy, his eating and drinking, his patience, his gratitude, his friendship, his love, his sleep, his prayer.

And we can contemplate the wonder of his awareness that one day he would live this summer and all days in you and me.

Come Apart and Rest With Me

> The apostles rejoined Jesus and told him all they
> had done and taught. Then he said to them, "You
> must come away to some lonely place all by your-
> selves and rest for a while," for there were so many
> coming and going that the apostles had no time
> even to eat.
>
> Mark 6:30-31

When was the last time you spent a week with
Jesus? Imagine a week — seven sunrises and seven
sunsets — resting with Jesus, perhaps wrestling
with him a bit, becoming reacquainted with him,
with yourself. Like Eucharist, a retreat is a time
of remembrance, a time to experience unity and
continuity.

Taking time to remember is a rare thing
these days. Most people never do this. In failing
to do so they diminish the depth to which they can
truly live the present. Our present is really the past
meeting the future. There is no such thing as living the present moment unrelated to the past and

future. That is too shallow and narrow an existence. What gives depth to the present moment is the whole reality of the past. This enables us to begin to recognize the patterns in our own lives, to begin to discern future directions.

What has happened in and to you throughout the past year, or the past ten years? What have been your moments of grace, of contemplation, of temptation? There is a cycle of grace that manifests itself in our lives in people who speak to us, events that happen around us, things we do in our world.

So often, people are not aware of these movements in their lives, of the ongoing development of their lives. We need time to recognize the rhythms and the movements. What expectations do I have of myself? How do I experience the sense of destiny within myself? It is reassuring to recognize that there is growth and movement within our lives, that new potentials and possibilities exist that were unseen before. It is challenging to miss a certain sense of direction or to discover a whole area of frustration.

A retreat provides a valuable opportunity for examining one's stance before God. We might look back to see the consistency of our good intentions, repeating patterns of failure, times we have been surprised by the Spirit. We might look at our portrait of Jesus, the image we carry with us today as distinguished from last year.

To retreat is always a time of knowing ourselves that we may know Christ, and of knowing Christ that we may know ourselves. To retreat is to take times of reflection, to pray rather than to analyze, to open oneself more fully to the Spirit. We cannot learn this deeply enough. In some way, this is all one has to do: to remember and to realize who Jesus is in order to know who we are.

There is never a time when we can say we are over the peak, we are done. The most precious moments are surely ahead of us. We need to be sensitive to the great power that is in Jesus. He will be with us forever doing all he can in us. If we could imagine the whole world coming into blossom through one tree, we might have a way to think of each one of us drawing upon the Body of Christ.

I once saw a banner with four trees, or more accurately the same tree at different seasons. The spring tree had buds upon it. The summer tree had the fruit. The leaves were falling from the autumn tree. The winter tree was stark — nothing remained. Yet it held my attention. The noblest tree of all has borne all it can bear, has emptied and exhausted itself so there is not one more blossom, not one more fruit, not one more falling leaf... and it seems to radiate a glow. Is this not what we are called to do?

We must see ourselves as more than ourselves. We must be aware of our deeper roots that enable us to draw on all of history. We must see this mysterious power that is within us. This is what Christ invites us to. We do not need to worry about our sins, our weaknesses, incapacities or inabilities. We just need to affirm the power of the Holy Spirit working within us. More than anything else, we need to believe with an almost unbelievable capacity in the power of Christ, in the presence of Christ, in what he can do in the least of us.

A retreat is a good time also to review our sense of the church, the community of the people of God. How are we affected by a community and in turn affect that community? Community is never established totally and completely because we are never finished as individuals. Community is really a matter of learning how to live, how to love together as persons. We are always open to further growth, and through this growth we discover the infinite possibilities of Christ in our lives. Each one of us is an extension of Jesus and we need to discover this in order to become more fully ourselves, to enable others to become more fully themselves.

When was the last time you spent a week with Jesus? Do you reverence yourself enough to offer yourself the gift of time with the One who calls you to dwell in his heart, with the One who dwells within your own heart? When will we know the immensity of God? Nothing can get outside of God. Everything exists within him. From all eternity each of us existed within his heart. He brought us forth in time and beyond time. He takes us back into his own heart.

Each of us is, was, will be within him as the stars of the night are within the cosmos and the expanding universe. Each of us is an expanding universe; we are the expanding universe of God. The universe breathes to the breath of God! This moment of my life recedes back into all the moments of my life, to that moment of my infancy held in the hands of the Father in the moment of his begetting me out of the infinity of his heart. A retreat can be a window and mirror into the universe and into the heart of Abba.

Relationship With God

We know that by turning everything to their good God cooperates with all those who love him, with all those that he has called according to his purpose. They are the ones he chose specially long ago and intended to become true images of his Son, so that his Son might be the eldest of many brothers. He called those he intended for this; those he called he justified, and with those he justified he shared his glory.

Romans 8:28-30

The prayer of the heart in the Eastern tradition of spirituality is a mantra prayer, a prayer of repetition, a prayer of scripture, the prayer of the blind man on the road to Jericho and the tax collector in the temple: "Lord, Jesus Christ, Son of God, have mercy upon me, a sinner."

The Eastern tradition of the prayer of the heart is a prayer of recognition of the depths of Christ's presence in us, a prayer of taking the thought and word from the lips and head on its journey into the heart until it radiates to every fiber of our being so that we almost become incandescent. It is a prayer of consecration uttered within the human heart.

Often this is called the Jesus Prayer. And in the scriptures we see other times and situations when Jesus prayed and showed his disciples how to pray. But the ultimate prayer of Jesus is the Eucharist. The ultimate prayer of Jesus is: "This is my body given for you; this is my blood to be shed for you." I think the most important command of Jesus to all of us is not simply to say this but *"Do this in memory of me."*

We must become his body broken, his blood spilled out for the life of the world. We have learned well his invitation to come and celebrate. It is only in our day that we are beginning to hear his command to go out and be the sacrament of liberation, the sacrament of reconciliation, the sacrament of salvation for the whole world.

We are beginning to recognize that his word over bread and wine is rendered ineffectual unless we dare to lay ourselves on the line, unless we dare to utter that prayer, that these bodies of ours are given not simply to him, but to the world. Jesus never asked us to follow Peter or Paul or John, but he said always and everywhere, "Follow *me.*"

He never tells us where we are going. And every time we approach the Eucharist, we are asked to say our amen. Augustine in the fifth century told his people, "Amen is a Hebrew word. We must translate it into our own language and amen says *Yes, I am the body of Christ.*" If only we could believe the truth of the Eucharist! The new kind of prayer is not new, except to us. It is the old prayer of Jesus, eternally new, giving himself totally and completely.

Sacraments must reach beyond the narrow boundaries we sometimes set on faith. So often our own contemporaries — the artists, the philosophers, the writers — somehow hear what the Spirit is doing in the world, long before those of us secure in the institutional church. A young French philosopher, Simone Weil, had utter faith in the Eucharist and utter faith in Christ but she did not become a Catholic because of her Jewish confreres who were dying in the concentration camps. She felt compelled to eat no more than they, and thus literally starved to death. With her own life she witnessed to Jesus' command to consecrate our body and blood for the salvation of the world.

I like the Western tradition of the Jesus prayer — that all of us are called not simply to be at the Eucharist, but that we are called to become Eucharist. All of us are called in some way to the melting point of Christ's love; we are called into a new depth of prayer that perhaps previous generations have not known, but which becomes essential for the work and the mission of the church today.

Christian prayer begins when we recognize that it is impossible to pray like Jesus unless we are through him, with him, and in him. The atomic scientists of our day perhaps lend us a vocabulary. They speak about fusion, of compression so immense that it releases an energy that has never been experienced in the world before. In the same way we recognize that within each of us is a hidden power, a hidden self, a hidden prayer that can never be released except through the presence of Jesus.

Scripture is more than a word about God; every word of scripture is always consecrating, always releasing immense energy. It is not simply revealing God to his people but revealing to us who we are in God, and who we are to become. Jesus gave his life that we might have this relationship with God and he tells us to continue this immense work in our own life.

The prayer of the Eucharist is a prayer of the heart. It is a mystical prayer in the ancient sense of the word. It is hidden. It cannot be touched or felt or seen. It is something that involves the act of God himself, the act of recognizing that God is Abba. But if we only think of father we have only half understood that word. It is a relational word. And if "father" embraces the terms son and daughter, it also implies brother and sister. I think we have heard the word Abba at last, but we are only beginning to hear the words brother and sister.

The prayer of the heart is a prayer not simply of an "I-thou" relationship, but a prayer that reaches out to our brothers and sisters whom we do not recognize, whom we have not known. The Eucharist is our way of doing this. We become one with Christ who reaches out to his brothers and sisters through us.

We are called to bear witness to the uniqueness of the prayer of the incarnation — Christ *does* make a difference and in him all things are created new. He calls us not simply to be divine, but he calls us to be as human as he is, which creates a whole new horizon for the human person.

Pathways Into Eucharist

The Eucharist is the invitation to remember. We are always being dismembered; we are always being fragmented. We must gather the fragments together and we must remember who we are; otherwise we will forget the journey.

Edward Farrell
Can You Drink This Cup?

The Eucharist is a gathering of Jesus' disciples to be at his table, to sit at his feet like Mary in Bethany, to rest their heads on his heart like John, to climb the mountain of the transfiguration like Peter, James and John, to be with him in prayer during his agony in the Garden of Gethsemane, to breakfast with him on a Galilean beach, to listen to his voice inviting us to come and rest, to listen, to eat, drink and be holy.

We enter into the church, that holy sanctuary, and we move into a higher level of consciousness, in touch with the mystery. We sign ourselves with the sign of our faith, the cross, and the waters of baptism. We make a sign of reverence before the fire of the sanctuary lamp, the burning bush of God's presence.

The first act of contemplation is reverence, the awareness of God. We enter into his silence and we pray. In recognizing his holiness, his goodness, and his love, we recognize our own sinfulness and cry out, "Lord have mercy." We ask him to cleanse and purify his temple in us. We so easily let it be filled with thieves who steal our identity, meaning and value. We forget who we are and whose we are.

But Jesus never lets us stay with our sin, brooding and nursing the pain of alienation. He is always saying to us the words of the loving father to prodigal children: "Celebrate and rejoice for this son of mine was dead and has come back to life; this daughter of mine was lost and is found."

Our joy erupts in the Gloria because we are in our Father's house and we are home to stay. Here we can rest and celebrate the new life we have been called to live.

"The Lord be with you. Let us pray." This is the great refrain, the continuous melody, inviting our presence before the indwelling Trinity. Father, Son and Holy Spirit have empowered us to pray and Jesus tells us over and over again that he hears us when we cry out to him.

Prayer opens us to God. It compels us to be

present to ourselves and to one another. Prayer leads us into a new silence, a new readiness, a new expectancy. Prayer creates this depth of silence in our hearts for the word to become flesh in us.

The word of God renders him present and renders us present to ourselves in a new way. The word of God carries his spirit and stirs up the grace of his cumulative deposit in us and we cry out "I believe."

We believe in God — Father, Son and Holy Spirit. We witness with our lives, with our stewardship of talent, time and treasure, that we are a sacrament of salvation for the whole world.

The first half of the eucharistic liturgy is a communal celebration of the first half of the Lord's Prayer: reverence, mercy, joy, prayer, word, faith. We remember, we celebrate, we hope, we dream, we believe, we offer.

The second half is Jesus' response to our gifts and prayers, the prayer of the faithful people of God who have gathered here. *Give* us *this day our daily bread....* Give us our daily joy and hope and friends, all that we need to fulfill our deepest needs. *Forgive us our sins....* Forgive our family, our city, our world as *we forgive those who have sinned against us....* In learning to forgive more completely we draw ever closer to God.

And lead us not into temptation.... We really mean well, but so often we forget, we wander off, get lost, and no longer know the way that leads to eternal life. Do not let us lead ourselves into temptation. We so easily avoid the light and are so often fascinated with the darkness and our own shadow. *Deliver us from the evil one.*

What of my life do I bring to the altar? How much needs to be blessed and consecrated? "What return can I make to Yahweh for all his goodness to me" (Ps 116:12). To offer is to cry out "Come, Lord Jesus." Come into my heart, my mind, my body and soul. Live in me and let me live in you.

To offer is to recognize my emptiness, my hunger, my poverty, to kneel in awareness of my own nothingness. To truly offer is to recognize that I have nothing to offer, nothing to give that is not already his gift to me. God cannot fill what is already full. We must be empty if we are to receive God fully in our lives. As Jesus abandoned himself so totally to the Father and to each one of us, so he invites our response, invites us to abandon ourselves to him, and through him, with him and in him to one another and to the world.

Eucharistomen — Giving Thanks

> Let us give thanks to the Lord our God.
> It is right to give him thanks and praise.
> Father, all-powerful and ever-living God,
> we do well always and everywhere to
>   give you thanks
> through Jesus Christ our Lord.
>
>   Order of the Mass

The Eucharist is our deepest act of self-identification with Jesus. He is always present, always ready to give himself to us and draw us more deeply into his hidden presence in ourselves and one another. Each one of us is at a different moment in our entering his life and his life entering into us. Each of us brings a different world for him to take, bless, break open and give back.

Jesus consecrated his own life in the Eucharist and he invites us to do the same with our lives. No one can do it for us — not the priest, not the community, not even Jesus. No one owns our lives like we do. No one can touch our freedom; we do with it what we choose. The decision, the consecration, the transformation of our lives depends on us.

Peter, John, James and the other apostles had to make their own decision to follow Jesus and eventually say, "This is my body given for you; this is my blood to be shed for you." The Eucharist is the great offering, this immense decision we must make again and again, every week and every day.

We need one another to stir up the hidden presence of Jesus in our inner selves. We need the energy, the faith, the hope, the love of one another. The Eucharist can never be done alone. If the people do not gather, the Eucharist cannot happen. In coming together through the Spirit we remember, we put together again, the body of Christ. Together we are the Body of Christ. And we remember so intensely that Jesus himself is present: "Wherever two or three are gathered in my name, there I am."

Jesus calls us together and enables us to experience more deeply the gifts we have already received. He calls us together so that we can celebrate the Eucharist over our lives and our world. He comes to us in his risen presence to empower us with the same Spirit that he was given. He takes, blesses, breaks and returns us. Then he sends us as he was sent to make disciples of all the people we touch in our daily world.

Jesus did not give us the Eucharist to hide himself on our altars or in our tabernacles. These are but momentary resting places, halfway points on his way into us and through us into the everyday world.

Each Sunday we come to believe and understand more deeply that Jesus is with us, in us, between us. Each of us is a sacrament, a hidden presence of Jesus, a Eucharist, carried into every street, factory and office. Jesus is present in the world because we are present.

How to Live Eucharist

Take this, all of you, and eat it:
this is my body which will be given up for you.
Take this, all of you, and drink from it:
this is the cup of my blood,
the blood of the new and everlasting covenant.
It will be shed for you and for all
so that sins may be forgiven.
Do this in memory of me.

Order of the Mass

What a strange request Jesus gave his disciples, a request he also gives to us, who are his special disciples in this community "Do this in memory of me." Jesus did not say "repeat these words after me." He said *do* this.

We have been faithful to "going to Mass" but now the Spirit is leading us to a deeper meaning of doing and living out the Eucharist, a depth of significance Jesus began at the Last Supper and completed on Good Friday and Easter Sunday.

The Eucharist is the fullest revelation and

manifestation of who Jesus is for us at this moment in our life and history. The Eucharist is our identity, the mirror of who we are and who we are becoming. The Eucharist is Christ, risen from the dead, living in our midst, leading us in our daily work of overcoming the darkness, joylessness and loneliness of the world through the light of the Gospel, the joy of the Eucharist, and the warmth of the community.

Jesus did not build himself a house and shut himself off from the world. He was a man of the streets, of the open roads. He was always trying to teach his disciples more, wanting them to understand more, leading them farther than they ever wanted to go. Jesus was always pushing and drawing his disciples further. They were always reluctant and hesitant, mumbling and grumbling among themselves. Sounds familiar, doesn't it?

The Eucharist is a journey. Jesus is always going on ahead of us. Jesus is leading us up the mountain of prayer where he wants to reveal himself to us. Life is movement, change, growth.

Jesus is always leading us to the altar, surrounded by the candles that are the symbol of the burning bush, the fire of God's presence. He invites us to drink of the well of God's word, a deep well that is never exhausted. And we join him at the table to feast on the bread and wine of his presence.

The Eucharist is not something we simply go

to. It must be more than something we attend. It is not something the priest does for us. The Eucharist is the deepest and most demanding personal experience of our spiritual lives. It demands a total active presence to ourselves or we will fail to recognize Jesus' total presence to us.

The Eucharist is a meeting with Jesus, an experience of God. That is why we call it a sacrament, a mystery — like the noonday sun, so bright that we cannot look into it for more than a second, or like the ocean, so immense that we cannot exhaust it. The Eucharist is the mystery of love, of violence, of death, of forgiveness and new life.

How can I show God that I love him, that everything I am is a gift from him? There are few dramatic moments of heroic witness. Perhaps the most important thing we have to offer is our fidelity — being here, believing, hoping, loving. We aren't always aware of our fidelity to self, family, friends, neighbors, work, church. But Jesus wants us to understand, to receive ever more fully the power of his Spirit, to enable our hidden inner selves to grow strong. The Eucharist could be the most conscious, deliberate, decisive hour of our day, of our week.

Corpus Christi — Body of Christ

> "I am the vine, you are the branches.
> Whoever remains in me,
> with me in him,
> bears fruit in plenty;
> for cut off from me you can do nothing."
>
> John 15:5

This is more than a mere figure of speech. Jesus knew how radically his disciples would have need of his breath, his spirit, his word, his food and drink. We might see this radical need in our contemporary astronauts with their umbilical cords of oxygen. It would be easier to live in outer space without oxygen than to follow Jesus in ministry without Eucharist.

It was impossible for us to climb up to God, so God has come down to us. He has scaled himself to our size, knocks at our door, comes to us under the form of bread. He has become so human, so close, so intimate, that the risk now is to overlook, to forget "the mystery hidden for centuries past and now revealed to us" (cf. Col 1:26).

The Eucharist is a universal prayer, the prayer of the multitudes, the way of union for the simple, the humble, the little children who know their Abba. Perhaps it is because the Eucharist is so ordinary that it is easily taken for granted.

Jesus gives us his own words to pray: "Give us this day our daily bread," and then he fulfills our prayer, fills our hunger with his body and blood. Some things are beyond the power of words to express. This is why he took bread, broke it and gave it to us. That bread and wine is the totality of his love, his death, his resurrection.

Jesus does not wait until we go into the desert or are led up a mountain. He meets us at the parish church. Wherever we gather together, he fulfills his promise to make his home in us. No longer do we have to lift our eyes to heaven, for God truly lives in us. The Eucharist teaches us to accept the presence of someone not myself in myself; the very giver of the being that I am.

His presence is not just a personal presence, but a mystical hidden union. We are somehow in him; he is in us. "I am in my Father and you in me and I in you" (Jn 14:20). This permanent union with Christ is the mystery of the faith which we proclaim, the mystery of the love which the Eucharist renders visible each day. What is deepest is invisible to the eye and can be touched only in contemplation.

The depths of the praying church are like treasure hidden in a field. We must make an investment before we can be sure of the treasure. The Eucharist, the praying church, is the pulsating heart of the universe. This mystery of the praying church opens up a new experience of God to ourselves. What incredible communion with divine life!

For Jesus, the Eucharist was more than a prayer, it was the whole of his life, the totality of his love being poured out for those he loved. His whole life was and is Eucharist, and it is into this totality that he calls us as his disciples.

Jesus' life was about carrying divine life to others, divine life so deep that it will always be hidden. Jesus' humanity gives depth to human life and enables us to be as human as he is. Yet Jesus is dependent upon our presence to him today. He can be present to others only through his cumulative presence in us. He alone has the power to touch the hardest of hearts. The Eucharist makes us new dimensions of the Body of Christ. The human presence of God in Christ — Incarnation, Eucharist — now continues in us. He draws us gradually into the universal consciousness, into his identity with all people.

The Eucharist becomes our window on the world, our door of union with the other human beings who inhabit the earth. The Eucharist is ultimately shared prayer, the communal experience, the corporate contemplation of the entire world. He has given us bread from heaven that we might become bread for the world.

The Cross — Mine, Yours, Ours

"If anyone wants to be a follower of mine let him renounce himself; take up his cross every day, and follow me."

Luke 9:23

The heart of Christianity is a cross, the sign of a love unto death, and beyond into resurrection. I am beginning to understand that there is no way of following Jesus except by undergoing what he underwent. Unless I die, I can never bear fruit.

No one in this world can escape suffering, but not all suffering is the cross. Suffering cannot be avoided, but one can escape the cross. The cross must be a choice, a free decision, or it is not the sign of Jesus' love. The cross is an invitation; each person must say yes. No one becomes a disciple without saying yes to Jesus taking us, blessing us, breaking us open, and passing us around.

Simone Weil wrote,

Love is a divine thing. If it enters the human heart, it breaks it. The human heart was created in order to be broken this way. It is the saddest waste if it is broken by anything else, but it prefers to be broken by anything rather than by divine love. Divine love breaks only those hearts which consent to be broken and this consent is difficult to give.

To be Christian, to be disciples, we must deliberately choose to be broken. To embrace him is to embrace the cross. The consequence of following Jesus is to carry the cross for oneself; for others, for the world.

Sometimes we need to reflect on these crosses we carry in our world. They are not always as obvious as the wooden cross Jesus carried to Calvary.

The cross of discipleship —
    inward struggle with the world,
      the flesh and the devil
    wrestling with laziness and inertia...
    so easy to take the less difficult path
    so comfortable to join the crowd,
    to do what
      everyone else is doing

The cross of fidelity —
    to inner vocation
    to hidden grace
    to unused talent
    to making decisions
    to saying yes or no

The cross of growth —
> of the pilgrim journey
> of the uphill climb
> with temperament and personality
> of conversion after relapse

The cross of ministry —
> taking the initiative of leadership
> giving of one's self to others

The cross of caring —
> involvement
> listening
> generosity

The cross of responsibility for others —
> those who turn to us
> those we would like to turn away from

The cross of our times —
> racism
> war
> poverty
> fear
> violence
> nuclear threat

Under the sign of this cross I pray:

In the name of the Father...

I touch my hand to my head, recognizing that I share in the very intelligence of the Father, who is loving me into existence at this very moment; the Father who draws me into eternal truth and ultimate values through his eternal wisdom and order in all creation; his personal providence in my life calling me by name and giving me my daily bread.

and of the Son…

I touch my hand to my heart, remembering Jesus' promise that he will take away my heart of stone and give me a heart of flesh — knowing that he has a human heart always inviting me to learn from him, for he is gentle and humble of heart, forgiving my sins and asking me to be his healing presence for others.

and of the Holy Spirit…

I touch my shoulders leading to my hands asking the Spirit to energize my whole body and being, that I dare to believe and hope that God's power working in me can do infinitely more than I can ask or imagine.

Amen.

Welcoming the Resurrection

"I am the resurrection.
Whoever believes in me, even though he
    dies he will live,
and whoever lives and believes in me
    will never die.
Do you believe this?"

John 11:25-26

Jesus asks us if we believe and we say yes, know-ing how little we understand. We know we touch the miracle of Easter life in baptism, pondering what can happen in an instant. The quantum leap from nothingness to life in the moment of birth, of consciousness, of faith, of love — such is the mystery of baptism, of resurrection.

Year after year the cycle of Easter passes over us. Or perhaps we pass through it. In the process something filters through to us, something is de-posited in us. The word of God pierces to the mar-row of the soul. It slips into our perception and if it cannot command us, it nevertheless haunts us with its subtle ways of nudging, drawing, grasping.

What was the resurrection like for Jesus? This is a healthy question, one which springs from the curiosity of living faith. Ordinarily scripture is very reserved in its expression of the great mysteries, and theology is limited by the reticence of scripture. But even so the word of God beckons us to stretch our imaginations and hearts.

The human fascination with the resurrection does not diminish, for it is the central reality of our faith, the fulfillment of our greatest hope and dream. Every person desires to believe in the resurrection, while at the same time being held back by a most anguishing kind of fear: What if it is not real? The nonbeliever cries out, "If only it were true!" The believer with no less difficulty cries out, "I believe, Lord. Help my unbelief!"

The synoptic gospels painfully emphasize the three distinct predictions and prophecies which Jesus made of his death and resurrection. The refrain is the same: They did not understand. John's gospel points out that right up until they were confronted with the empty tomb, they were confused and unsure of the meaning of his words: "Till this moment they had failed to understand the teaching of scripture, that he must rise from the dead" (Jn 20:9).

Mark's gospel is blunt about the disciples' reaction to the first witness of the Risen Jesus: "But they did not believe her when they heard her say that he was alive and that she had seen him" (Mk 16:11) and again with the Emmaus travelers, "these went back and told the others, who did not believe them either" (Mk 16:13). And finally he writes that Jesus showed himself to the eleven when they were at table and "reproached them for their incredulity and obstinacy, because they had refused to believe those who had seen him after he had risen" (Mk 16:14).

Luke is more gentle as he describes that Easter evening when he stood in their midst and asked them: "'Why are you so agitated? And why are these doubts rising in your hearts? Look at my hands and feet; yes, it is I.' Their joy was so great, they could not believe it and they stood there dumbfounded" (Lk 24:38-41). Here it is not stubbornness prompting their lack of belief but confusion and surprise and the joy of their desires seeming to be fulfilled. They hardly dared to believe the wonder of it.

Our belief is much like that of the apostles. We want to believe but sometimes we refuse because we fear disappointment. And sometimes we simply can't believe because the joy seems too great to bear. And at times we would like to have some physical, tangible proof. Yet we know that we must have faith in what Jesus told Thomas: "You believe because you can see me. Happy are those who have not seen and yet believe" (Jn 20:29).

Still, we envy the women coming away from the tomb: "There, coming to meet them, was Jesus" (Mt 28:9). What a moment! And here again when we would most like a few words of detail, the scripture is reticent in a grand silence. Yet what could we say? What could we understand more than that understanding already given to us?

Nevertheless, even after all these years of celebrating his resurrection, I am sure our human curiosity has endless questions ready for our own "third day." For what is of greater human interest to us than his resurrection? What did he experience in his human consciousness? What were his thoughts and feelings as he rolled up the shroud in which he had been wrapped?

The experience of human consciousness from Adam to Christ — how much history is involved? Is the memory of that first moment buried in our collective unconsciousness? But who among us can remember even those first conscious processes in our individual life stories? Who among us could begin to know the unhindered fullness of Christ's consciousness in the resurrection until such time as we enter into his eternal consciousness ourselves?

All the great moments of history and human achievement — the discovery of fire, tools, agriculture, the development of language, art, literature, the invention of the engine, airplanes, rockets, atomic energy, space travel — pale before the moment of Christ's resurrection. All of history and eternity are changed in that first moment of the human consciousness of the risen Christ. He had overcome the world.

What must have been the joy in the human heart of Jesus! What must have been the peace smile on his face! He must have known immense joy and peace in the unfolding of all that he had tried to say and do: redemption and resurrection of the whole world, humankind's freedom unbent, heaven opened, sin and death overcome, the unity of humankind inaugurated, the hopes and dreams of all the centuries realized, all men and women freed from their inability to love.

Creation, standing on tiptoe, began to experience the new Spirit of life breathed and poured forth over all humankind. One can imagine the fullness of Jesus as he experienced the inexpressible gratitude of men and women for all time slowly growing to an awareness and a conviction of resurrection with Christ.

His Spirit is being released over all of humankind; truth, joy and peace are being poured into us. All that is human is externalized; all that is divine is now ours in him. He is to be with us always, giving us a taste of what he is now, what we will become. He is drawing us into himself. Now he is ever present; he will not leave us friendless. Before the resurrection he was limited by bodily space to one house, one city, one person, one group at a time. No longer is he confined to a limited circle of human presence. He comes fully to all those who desire and love him.

We are witnesses to the resurrection no less than the apostles and Paul, for the risen Christ can be known only in faith. No one recognized what appeared before their senses. The only Jesus we can believe in is the risen Lord who draws us to himself, giving us his Spirit, enabling us to believe. If we believe, it is through his Spirit. The Spirit in us enables us to see the glory of the resurrection, the quiet hidden glory of his annunciation, birth, life and death now continued in water, bread and wine, oils, human words and hands, the sacraments of everyday which transform us into a sacrament of Jesus.

Easter life! One moment of life would have been enough, one moment of love, of consciousness, of truth, of joy. But we are called to live all these moments without end. His resurrection has begun the parousia; the world to come is here; the kingdom is in our midst.

The Call to
Be Disciple and Friend

"I shall not call you servants any more,
because a servant does not know
his master's business;
I call you friends,
because I have made known to you
everything I have learnt from my Father."

John 15:15

I would like to invite people of faith to share their experience of Jesus, so I begin with my own: I think of myself as a friend of Jesus, spending time with him, thinking about him, recognizing his presence, knowing and experiencing that he loves me, seeing my life through his eyes.

He has been with me all the days of my life. I have never been alone. He is my companion. He is with me when I wake up in the morning; he is with me as I prepare myself for the day. He knows what I feel because he had to get up every morning. And I am sure that on some mornings he had no more desire to get up than I do.

He is with me as I get my breakfast. He got his own breakfast more often than not. Scripture mentions that he made breakfast for the disciples after the resurrection along the shore of the sea of Galilee.

Jesus worked with his hands. He was a carpenter, which in his days probably meant a stonecutter. He had to work with hard material like fieldstone. It must have been exhausting work, demanding a strong back and much muscle.

Jesus did not have his own business. He could not pick and choose his own hours and his own kind of work. Jesus was an employee. He was just another anonymous worker. No one noticed him. Everyone was astounded when he began to preach and teach in his own synagogue.

I am always amazed at how ordinary Jesus' life is. And at the center of his life he placed a great deal of importance on friendship with those around him. The first thing he did when he began his ministry was to gather a community of friends.

Jesus always initiates friendship with us. Only Jesus dares to share everything with each of us, and to invite us to share everything with him. Many people simply followed Jesus, sometimes at a distance, sometimes with suspicion, sometimes timidly, afraid to get involved. But his closest friends and disciples were called. They were invited to share their lives with him. And he still invites people to be friends with him today. How do people respond?

Among our own acquaintances we can see that some are like Nicodemus. They are drawn to Jesus by curiosity or spiritual hunger, yet are hesitant to go public. They come by night, in secret, so as not to be seen by others. Others, drawn by that same fascination, resist the attraction, try to suppress the call, laugh it off and make light of anything to do with Jesus. Are we embarrassed to call Jesus our friend? It is good to know he understands, that he will take any opportunity to listen to our questions, to answer them so that we might begin to understand. But it's difficult to nourish a genuine friendship in secret like this.

Some honest people have truly been scandalized by those who call themselves friends of Jesus and go to church on Sunday but betray Jesus in their everyday behavior. These scrupulously honest ones try to be faithful to Jesus but never go to church lest they be identified with those whom they consider to be hypocrites. They expect too much of the Christian and forget that the church is a community of sinners. They forget that Jesus was a friend to the tax collector who stood in the back of the temple confessing his sins. Not all churchgoers are unaware of their sins during the week. Perhaps we need this time, even if it's only an hour a week, to reflect on how we have failed our friend Jesus, how we might become better friends.

Of those who do go to church regularly, many keep up all their obligations but do not volunteer or become involved in parish activities.

They are the faithful servants who have not yet experienced their call to be friends, disciples, apostles. They are busy about their business, doing all that they think will make Jesus and his friends comfortable. Like Martha in Bethany they bustle about the church but never take time to sit at Jesus' feet and listen to his stories.

But the men and women who do become involved in the parish have usually experienced Jesus' special goodness, and want to make some return for all the ways in which he has blessed their lives. This is the response to the invitation to be a disciple, and even more to be a friend. They have followed Jesus when he invited them to his dwelling, they have offered him the hospitality and simple presence of friendship.

How does someone become a friend? One does not create a friend or choose to have a friend. A friend belongs to the realm of gift, of mystery, of the call to take off your shoes for you are on holy ground. Friendship seems to happen because of the quality of cumulative presence that builds up through the lapsed time shared with one another. This is how our friendship with Jesus grows.

The curious thing about our friendship with Jesus is that it draws us into a deeper friendship with other people around us. We begin to see that other people are friends with Jesus too. There is something of Jesus and his love in every person. This is the mystery of Eucharist.

Becoming a Disciple

"You did not choose me. No, I chose you; and I commissioned you to go out and to bear fruit that will last.... It is to the glory of my Father that you should bear much fruit and then you will be my disciples."

John 15:16, 8

Pentecost, the seventh day of the seventh week, is the New Creation, the outpouring of the Resurrection into each and all of us, the breathing of the Risen Christ in us that will never end! Paul reminds us again and again that "the depths of God can only be known by the spirit of God. Now instead of the spirit of the world we have received the spirit that comes from God to teach us to understand the gifts that have already been given us" (1 Cor 2:11-12).

The Acts of the Apostles are not finished. Our generation is living and writing new chapters. The word of God continues to unfold. The Book of Revelation dazzles our imagination and dares us to believe God when he says, "Now I am making the whole of creation new" (Rev 21:5). To balance, comprehend and integrate our century's discovery and exploration of outer and inner space, we are compelled to enter new depths of the spirit. Indeed, the Holy Spirit, as the poet Hopkins wrote, "Broods over the world with warm breath and with ah! bright wings."

Now in new ways Christian communities are beginning to recognize more fully the great and incredible working of the spirit. Does anyone adequately contemplate the great works of the Holy Spirit? Contemplation is more than theological understanding. To contemplate means to be drawn by the Spirit into the energy, power and mystery of what is happening and what we are becoming.

The special grace of our times is that more and more Catholics are experiencing a new understanding of their identity and call. Fewer are content to be passive members of the Sunday congregation. It is no longer enough to be anonymous *members* of a parish. Many are experiencing a need to be visible *disciples* of Jesus.

How does this conversion happen? Sometimes it is meeting the right person at the right time, which creates in us a desire to be like that person. Sometimes it is a meeting with other searching people. Many times it is reading a book, listening to a sermon, seeing a movie like *Gandhi*. Everyone has a gift and a talent. Something buried in us for half a lifetime suddenly comes to the surface, and we can no longer suppress it.

A disciple experiences a joy and peace so deep within that he or she is compelled to share it with others. When this hidden mission begins to emerge in us, we find other people who also know that they have been haunted by Jesus and are drawn to each other to grow together in him.

When we begin to follow Jesus, we allow him to live more consciously in our lives. In surprising and simple ways, he is always speaking to us. He is at the heart of the world and at the heart of each of us, especially at the fragile center where we are afraid — of ourselves, of others, of God. Fragile people are such a revelation of God.

We need to rediscover how to relate eye to eye, hand to hand, heart to heart. We have to encourage one another to keep walking toward joy, toward truth, toward God. We need one another to simplify our lives and to live where God is most to be found — in our deeper presence with each other. In order to do this we need to be purified, to be freed of excess baggage.

Jesus called into existence a community of disciples to follow him at extreme risk. A safe Christianity is not genuinely Christ-like. Christianity will always be counter-cultural, a protest culture. And this means that we must always dare to stand up for what we believe in, to commit ourselves to our beliefs in spite of the tension between being a believer and belonging to the secular culture.

We are responsible for the progress of the gospel we proclaim. Either tacitly or aloud, but always forcefully, we are being asked: Do you live what you believe? Do you really preach what you live? The witness of life has become more than ever an essential condition for real effectiveness in preaching.

The gospel message is not an optional contribution for the church. It is the duty incumbent on all Christians so that people can believe and be saved. This message is indeed necessary. It is unique. It cannot be replaced. It permits neither indifference nor accommodation.

Above all, the gospel must be proclaimed by the witness of a Christian life. Through this wordless witness, Christians stir up irresistible questions in the hearts of those who see how they live. Such a witness is already a silent proclamation of the Good News and an effective one. Here we have an initial act of evangelization. Who are the Christians who give such witness? The ones who hear and live the invitation of Jesus.

Living More With Less

"If you wish to be perfect, go and sell what you own and give the money to the poor, and you will have treasure in heaven; then come, follow me."
                                    Matthew 19:21

Living More With Less is the title of a book that I have been reading. It was written by Doris Jansen Longacre. The core of this book is personal testimonies of ordinary people all over the world who have experienced the need for a more simple way of living. Five "life standards" emerge from these contributions: Do justice, learn from the world community, nurture people, cherish the natural order and non-conform freely.

Our stewardship, sharing together our treasure, time and talent, keeps vibrating strongly in me this theme of living more with less. The American Dream of the pursuit of happiness in our consumer culture becomes a pursuit of affluence, with the illusion that the more we have, the better we live and are. This hunger and drive for more is not only a temptation but a subtle and dangerous addiction.

Possessions tend of themselves toward obsession. The good things of life have a strange fascination and power over the human heart. Beautiful things can be so attractive and promise-filled. We are so conditioned and drawn into envy by what others have, by what we want, by the advertising that tells us we deserve all these things.

We are hardly aware of their constant enticement, seduction and entrapment. The thought becomes a desire; the desire becomes a need; the need becomes a necessity; then I will do anything, pay any price, to have it. And when I finally do have it, in a deeper sense I discover that it has me.

We begin, sometimes without realizing it, to worship things, to relate to them as persons. And in the process, we inevitably relate to other persons as if they were things.

No wonder Jesus spoke five times as often about money and earthly possessions as about prayer. And everywhere in scripture we hear the warnings: money has power; wealth is addictive. Be careful, be on your guard.

Does anyone fear wealth as much as poverty? For a disciple of the gospel is wealth even more dangerous than poverty? Today such questions are coming not only from monasteries and religious communities but from lay people.

When God breaks in on a sufficiently prepared people, a new generosity emerges, one that is outgoing, joyous, spontaneous and free. Growth in Christian discipleship manifests itself by compassion for the poor. A new stewardship unfolds, a stewardship that cares deeply for all of God's created order, including the earth and its fullness — people, animals and things.

Our first American saint, Elizabeth Ann Seton, prayed "to live more simply so that others may simply live." Our lives as disciples should reflect this concern for others. Jesus told his disciples:

> "Anyone who wants to be great among you must be your servant, and anyone who wants to be first among you must be your slave, just as the Son of Man came not to be served but to serve."
>
> Matthew 20:26-28

Journeys of Mary — Journey of a Disciple's Heart

"Rejoice, Mary,
the Lord loves you very dearly.
He is with you!"

Luke and John are the evangelists of Mary. The oldest prayer of the Christian community has its beginning in Luke's gospel. The angel Gabriel announces to Mary that she is invited to be the mother of Jesus: "Hail Mary, full of grace, the Lord is with you" (cf. Lk 1:28). Mary goes in haste to visit her cousin Elizabeth, whose child leaped for joy in her womb. Elizabeth, filled with the Holy Spirit, cried out: "Blessed are you among women, and blessed is the fruit of your womb, Jesus" (cf. Lk 1:42). Ever since, the Christian community has echoed the prayers of Gabriel and Elizabeth and added its own unique refrain: "Holy Mary, Mother of God, pray for us sinners now and at the hour of our death."

Now and the hour of our death. These are the two ultimate moments of each person's life. Each time we pray these words, these moments come closer together and the journey grows shorter. It is good that we do not walk alone. It is important that we have a companion with us on our journey. What a joy and grace, then, to recognize that our journeys are linked with the journeys of Mary!

At the wedding feast at Cana, Mary's compassion found expression in the words "They have no wine." This is Mary's beautiful prayer for us. Wine is the symbol of joy. Mary always knows when we are running out of joy, running out of life. She anticipates Jesus' prayer for us "that my own joy may be in you and your joy be complete" (Jn 15:11).

She is always and foremost the first disciple of Jesus. Even from the cross, Jesus sent Mary on a journey that would last until the end of time, the journey into our hearts, the journey of being companion to his disciples, to be mother of the church as she was his mother.

What is our story of Mary? How does our generation in the twentieth century fulfill the prophecy to call Mary blessed? How is she fruitful in us? In her journeys let us recognize our journey, our story, our magnificat.

With the persistence of the ocean tides, the images and symbols of Mary rise again and again in the Christian consciousness. Every generation discovers anew for itself that God is born of a woman, that the one human person who is closest to and most like Christ is a woman, and that Mary is the ultimate expression of what is human and what is woman. In her the Christian community continues to discover all that God is doing in us.

The late '60's and '70's witnessed diminishment of traditional devotions to Mary just as the women's movement picked up momentum. We are still in the unfolding of women and the liberation of Mary. I like the new images of Mary that I see emerging today, a Mary identified with the oppressed and suffering women of our world, as well as with the women discovering new strength and grace in the call to be disciples.

Because we can never catch up to her, Mary will always be the most contemporary of women. For many, the new consciousness of woman is a new consciousness of Mary. We can only grow gradually into the fullness of Mary's humanity and personhood, her womanhood, her sisterhood.

She is already what we are beginning to be. Every new stage of our growth and evolution gives us a new self-understanding and thus, a new capacity to understand her. She must wait for us to liberate her; to free her from the images of our childhood and the church's past. These images, childhood images of the Christian community, will never be invalidated. But the seed must not be kept a seed; it must die and grow and bear fruit.

How significant it would be for each of us to recognize the journey of Mary into our hearts so that we can sing and dance our own magnificats, the stories of the wonderful things God has done and revealed to our heart and invited us to become. Mary's magnificat is a model and pattern for all Christian prayer as it expresses her presence to herself, to God, and to all God's people.

The magnificat tells of that threefold journey of discovery and love. Mary comes to know and love herself. She is unafraid of speaking openly about this self — "my soul... my spirit... he has looked upon me... all generations will call me blessed... the Almighty has done great things for me."

Out of Mary's profound presence to herself, receiving the gift and sacrament of who she is, she is compelled to dance and sing her gratitude and celebration of what God has done, is doing and will continue to do from age to age forever.

Out of her presence to God she is present to the *anawim,* the powerless and the voiceless, the hungry and those in need of help. She dares to prophesy that the proud of heart will be routed, the princes pulled down from their thrones, the rich sent empty away. God is faithful to his promises forever!

Being Welcomed Home

Jesus turned around, saw them following, and said, "What do you want?" They answered "Rabbi," — which means Teacher — "where do you live?" "Come and see," he replied; so they went and saw where he lived, and stayed with him the rest of that day.

John 1:38-39

Remember those experiences of being welcomed home? To know a place is to deposit your life there. Something of you is invested there forever. Our days and nights, our summers and winters, springs and falls, are lived in particular times and places. Something of us is absorbed there. It lives there and welcomes us back home.

We can merely survive almost any place, but to know and love ourselves, to live and grow, we need a special environment. We need to be at home in favorite places — rivers, lakes, hills, farms, city streets, small town shops, houses filled with memories of happy days. These special places can gentle us and comfort us and ultimately hold out infinity. The wind of memory can awaken the stars. I return to special places and people because a new experience, a new possibility has awakened me, or because something stirs the ghosts of ancestors within me.

I was with my father when he returned to his home in Ireland after twenty-eight years in Detroit. He remembered every bend in the winding country road, every little hill and farm, every line of trees and hedge row of field stones. He remembered so much more than the people who had continued to live there and had forgotten, caught up in the daily routine of merely surviving.

We lived in the same house where we grew up for over fifty years. I felt so well known by the trees and lawns, the convent school and church. They still hold all my years, giving back memories when I return for a visit.

Even more than places, special people carry the repository of our life, our elapsed time with them. By myself, I can never be known or even know myself as fully as I can be known through the presence of others. I have a sense that I am more present to myself with special friends than when I am entirely alone. I can never love myself as I am worth being loved. We need one another to bring out what is best in ourselves, what is hidden from us in our incompleteness.

We need times to experience and celebrate

the bonds of being with family, friends and relatives. We need an environment of acceptance, love, affirmation, kinship, at-home-ness with people who express their esteem, affection and appreciation of us. No energy need be expended in their presence. Rather we become energized by the very richness and depth of their presence. We need these expansive times to rest and relax, to be renewed in spirit. The experience of being drawn into the inner being of others, their inner space, their zone of freedom, peace, and joy is exhilarating.

The Eucharist has created in us a new capacity to be with others. Christ has opened a door in us that no one can close. We discover a new energy for others, energy for a new world and a new humanity. We are already one in Christ through his incarnation, death and resurrection. Eucharist is the continuing experience of being plunged into the inner being of God and of one another and becoming sacrament in and for the world. It is our way of being connected, of completing the circle of life, of being both nurtured and generative. It is the creative energy of water and seed.

My sense of being at home with others is nurtured by the recognition that it is good to take time to be at home with myself, with the experience of solitude. There is a presence in me deeper than my own presence, a prayer, an energy, a wisdom, a connectedness, a grounding that I have only inklings of — treasure buried in a field, a pearl of great price. There is something inside of me that can receive and respond to God. He draws me. He attracts me. He fills up my life. When you want to rest, to grow, to develop, shut the door, go into your inner being. Become present to the length and breadth, the height and depth within your self and you will learn, you will be reborn.

Immerse your being in God, in goodness, health and love, in beauty, joy and glory. You are God's work of art, his vineyard. There are no perfect days, yet there are perfect moments in each day. Treasure them! Treasure your connectedness with nature, with the universe, history, others, the whole world. Treasure going to the wellsprings where you are still being formed, still growing.

We need to be at home with ourselves, with others, with our God. When we discover our center and our connectedness, we come closest to sharing in the creating and forgiving power of God. Then we are always at home, no matter where we are, because God reveals his love by creating the home within me, within you, within all.

Jesus understood this rootedness, this need to be at home, when he told the disciples on the eve of his own going home to his Father:

> "There are many rooms in my Father's
> house;
> if there were not, I should have told you.
> I am going now to prepare a place for you,

and after I have gone and prepared you a
        place
I shall return to take you with me;
so that where I am
you may be too.
You know the place where I am going."
                                John 14:2-4

One day we, too, will be welcomed home.

Mother, Mary

As for Mary, she treasured all these things and
pondered them in her heart.

Luke 2:19

Sometime before her death, my mother had a
stroke and had to give up the family home. This
stirred many memories and I would like to share
my reflections on those memories with you.
Through her gentle companion presence, my
mother taught me much about Mary and Nazareth.

The first imprint my mother made was her
warm, gentle presence. Hospitality and gracious-
ness were the immediate responses to everyone
who entered her home. "Let me give you a little
something to eat and drink" were her actions rather
than her words. She was most comfortable serv-
ing and waiting on people, filling them to the full
and then some.

Mother had a great contentment for she lived
a simple life and had so few needs or wants. She

was grateful for whatever she had, because it always seemed more than she ever expected. She rarely ever spent on herself. Her generosity was to us, her children.

Listening was an art with her, and she had some simple wisdom for everyone who sought her counsel or support. I hope everyone has in his or her life a loving person who is free to be for others, a generous person who draws out our best qualities and quiets the negative and selfish voices within us.

She was an *anam chara*, which is Irish for soul friend. As individuals poured out their hearts to her, she listened, absorbed the pains and wounds and gave them peace and comfort in exchange. Her simple expressions carried great healing power because she lived in the depths of the Lord.

My mother reminds me in many ways of the woman the mother of Jesus must have been. Mary could not have been a "holy" person who makes other people uncomfortable and speechless. I am beginning to think of Mary as she advanced in age to what her cousin Elizabeth was when she carried John. Imagine Mary with wrinkles, but still with the smoldering fire of the Holy Spirit deep within her. She must have been the light and joy of the entire neighborhood, drawing so many to herself to experience a hint and hope of what lay ahead for them.

Mary must have lived each day so full of

grace, joy, peace and contentment that nothing
more could be added, poured into this moment,
this day.

We might offer this litany to Mary our
mother:

Woman
Mom
Mary of rattling tea cups and homemade
  cookies
Mary of open door, open hearth, open
  heart
Queen of warmth and hospitality
Mary of varicose veins and chapped hands
Strong, fragile woman
Vulnerable, unshakable woman
Believer in love, reality, people, God
Back stooped and ear bent in listening to
  life's stories and to the Giver of life
Stubborn fidelity to life in the face of death
Unflinching spirit that stares light into the
  darkness of the tomb
Heart that breaks and pours love over the
  thirsty earth
Missing her son when he is gone to
  another home
Looking up in the sudden expectancy of
  hearing his voice
Smiling wryly to herself and waiting

Waiting, gestating the kingdom once more
Growing in expectancy of second birth —
    this time her own
The moment of reunion rushes to meet her
    with open arms
And their laughter rocks the universe
Sending happy shock waves to echo in our
    dreams
Tugging our reluctant mouths into smiles
    of hope and anticipation
Amen, it will be so, Amen.

"I Am Not Going to Die"
— A Living Remembrance

A joy is full grown only when it is remembered. Joy and memory is all one thing. When you and I met the meeting was over very shortly, it was nothing. Now it is growing something as we remember it. But still we know very little about it. What it will be when I remember it as I lie down to die, what it makes in me all my days until then, is the real meeting. The other is only the beginning of it.

C.S. Lewis

I find myself reflecting on the Last Supper of Jesus. We seldom recognize a final occasion when it is happening. Only in retrospect do we recognize that it was the last. Then we recall every moment, every gesture and try to draw from it what we will carry with us the rest of our lives. So easily we take for granted the meals of every day. They are so regular and common, so ordinary as long as they continue. But when it is the last one, all of the previous ones are drawn into it and it becomes a singularity, a once and never again. It becomes a rare, precious moment to be treasured forever.

The disciples did not fully understand Jesus until he left them. Even at the first Eucharist, when they were so aware of him in their midst, seeing him, hearing him, touching him, they still couldn't fathom the depth to which he could be present to them. It was only afterward, when he gave them his body and blood, that they understood. He was no longer someone outside of them but rather he was within them in a whole new way, a new form of life!

An unfathomable core of uniqueness rests in the inner being of each individual. The closer and dearer the person is, the more difficult to express the mystery of that presence in our life. But very often the one who is closest to us in life is the one we never fully understand and appreciate.

My mother died recently at the age of ninety-one. It is surely a wonderful and awesome experience to sit and kneel by your mother, watching her being born to eternal life as she must have watched you being born into human life. All of her children surrounded her in the last hours, praying in a very quiet way.

Her own faith made it a particularly moving experience. For sixty years, living next to the church, she attended Mass and received communion each day. Prayer was a hunger in her! She loved to be in the house of the Lord, "to serve him in holiness and virtue in his presence" (Lk 1:75). When I had asked her if she was going to die, she answered, "I am not going to die." She was not going to die. She was not afraid. She was so sure. And before we realized it, she was born into new life. Breathing quietly, without a tremor or gasp, without a moment's break, she simply began to live a new life.

She bore witness to the reality that Jesus never experiences us as dead. We can only live in him and with him. She did not die; she simply entered his life. The warmth, the pulse, the breathing we were feeling as we held her was our own warmth, our own heartbeat, our own breath. No longer was she outside us; she was within! She was there as the pulse of our hearts.

Mother so fully deposited her presence in me, so wrapped me in her peace and joy and love without words, that I can only call that quality of presence eucharistic. She made tangible the great fruit of the Eucharist. Out of the Lord's presence in us, we come into a new kind of presence with one another that is truly sacramental.

And now, in drawing her into himself, Jesus reveals himself more fully to me. She is now present to me in the way Jesus is present to me in the Eucharist. In her dying and being born to new life, she is no longer outside of me, but inside — her breath, her pulse, her heartbeat, her spirit is in me. She lived her life as a prayer for her children and all those she loved. And God fulfilled her prayer by pouring out his love, kindness and tenderness to all those she carried in her heart.

And so it is we celebrated her resurrection Mass, more as a wedding than a funeral, with great joy, great peace, great fullness. We offered back to her all that she so generously, graciously and freely gave to us. The overflow and radiation of her presence continues to embrace all of those who carry the cumulative deposit of her life in their hearts, that we might draw closer to becoming the one body in Christ.

Death of a Spiritual Director

Remember your leaders, who preached the word of God to you, and as you reflect on the outcome of their lives, imitate their faith.

Hebrews 13:7

Monsignor William Lynch was my teacher, spiritual director, mentor and guide from the time I entered the seminary until his death in 1982. But more than all that he was my friend, as he was friend to so many others. His life ministry was to be a companion to people on their spiritual journey to the hidden reality and mystery of Jesus.

In reflecting on his death and on his life, I see how deeply he affected the lives of all who knew him. It suggests that the relationship we have with those who share the intimate moments of our spiritual and sacramental lives is profoundly moving.

What happens to the words of a priest? What happens to his prayer and penance? What becomes of his tears and heartbreaks? What happens to his life? I know what happened to Monsignor Lynch's life. He deposited something of his life in every person he met, seeds that would continue to grow and bear fruit. A priest like Monsignor Lynch doesn't die. He simply expends the last energy of his life. There is no more life in him because it has been totally given away. When life is poured out like this, then the spirit breaks out of the body and descends upon the barely remembered seeds implanted in many, and nurtures and stirs them to become fruitful thirty, sixty, a hundredfold.

I am sure that, like one of his favorite saints, Thérèse of Lisieux, he "intends to spend his eternity doing good upon earth." His life echoes the words of Teresa of Avila: "If you would progress a long way along the road, the important thing is not to think much but to love much."

It is a rare and wonderful experience to know a priest as a father, a spiritual friend, a brother, a companion! Monsignor Lynch's friends numbered in the hundreds. He had an ever-expanding capacity for friendship. He was a great conversationalist and storyteller; yet he was also an extraordinary listener. He listened almost too much, too deeply. In his presence, you were aware of silences you never experienced before.

He saw the best and the most dangerous in each person. He looked so deeply into people that he enabled them to discover depths and potential that had not yet been experienced. He called forth a goodness, a hope, a generosity from people that they rarely suspected lay hidden within them. He activated hidden latencies, enkindled new possibilities.

He was always "good news." He was a well, a fountain that gave deep refreshment. One could almost feel embarrassed by his unfeigned admiration and warm affection. You simply became more present to yourself because of his presence with you.

The sacrament of penance was his most distinctive ministry. No one will easily forget the experience of celebrating reconciliation with Monsignor Lynch. One could never leave his confessional or room without experiencing a tangible sense of the spirit of God. No matter how routine your confession might be or how unspiritual you might feel, when you left his presence you knew that something fresh and good had been stirred up within. Somehow you knew that you had walked and talked with God.

The Eucharist was the center of his life. Whenever he left his room, or the seminary, or the rectory, the first and last stop was always a visit to the Blessed Sacrament. Even the last time I took him home from the hospital, his first stop was a visit to the Eucharist. His spirituality was that of Berulle, Olier, Marmion, Chautard, Boylan — "Christ before my eyes; Christ in my heart; Christ in my hands."

He was not a brilliant or innovative thinker or preacher. He worked long and hard over each of his conferences, each of his talks. Many times he reminded me that it was the time and prayer you put into your talk that made it fruitful, not the delivery. He not only worked and prayed over what he was to say, but he contemplated the word of God so deeply that when he spoke of the love of Christ and the Eucharist, tears would flow down his face. As students we were embarrassed for him, or perhaps embarrassed for ourselves because we didn't understand.

He was an ordinary person with ordinary talents but because he put so much of himself into everything he did, and into every relationship he had, he became an extraordinary priest. He wrote no books, published no articles, started no movements, built no church buildings. He had the great grace of a parish priest, that rare "common touch" that made every ordinary person feel very special. In Monsignor Lynch we caught a glimpse, a touch of Jesus. He has carried much of each of us who knew him before our Father. We feel closer to the Lord because he carries us in his great heart. We must be confident that he will continue to spend his spirit to bring to fruition the seed that he has planted in us.

Sharing the Priesthood of Christ

> But you are *a chosen race, a royal priesthood, a consecrated nation, a people set apart* to sing the praises of God who called you out of the darkness into his wonderful light.
>
> 1 Peter 2:9

Part of being human is remembering who we are and daring to dream who we might become. What has become of me in living out thirty years of priesthood? Life has humbled me and I have become more simple, more wide-eyed, more childlike, more lost in mystery, more fascinated, more excited — yet in a quieter way. I am drawn more into prayer; the Eucharist haunts me more totally. Everything is gift and surprise. It draws more wonder and gratitude out of me. And all of this has come about because of the people God has brought into my life. I began my priesthood by offering my life to Christ and he has filled my life with his people. He told the apostles, concerned about the hungry multitudes, "Give them something to eat yourselves" (Mt 14:16). And more and more I am discovering the wisdom of this. The more I give, the more I receive; the more I teach, the more I learn; the more I minister, the more I am ministered to.

To be a priest is to be called to love each person as Jesus does. And to love is to see: to see Jesus in the other and give time, attention, care, presence, healing; to see each person as burning bush, fire of divine love, living flame; to see the hidden goodness and truth in each person, to see with the eye of the spirit that not only sees outer beauty but discerns inner goodness.

A priest should experience the presence of Christ so deeply and become so excited about this presence that he is compelled to share this gift, this secret, this mystery with others. In recent years we have seen a wonderful rediscovery of ministry. We have grown in the awareness that to be Christian is to be called into a ministry. We have awakened to the mystery of our share in Jesus' priesthood. Every one of us should experience what it is to be priest, to be chosen, to be loved, to be broken.

We are each called to a hidden priesthood over our life, our world, our time: consecrating, elevating, lifting up, energizing, loving, hallowing, transforming. We must learn to be creative with and in our lives, bringing our world to new birth and redeeming it. We must become artists, poets and musicians, transforming life into something holy and wonderful, pouring in new life, light, joy. Together with the creator of the universe, we must bless creation rather than curse it. He makes all things new through you and me, through our lives and our priesthood.

The sacramental priesthood builds upon a natural cosmic priesthood but at times we forget this fundamental reality. Every woman and man has a heart and spirit greater than the world and can contemplate the whole visible universe. Gathering it up within, he or she offers it, hallows it, consecrates it to the living invisible God. Each person offers what he or she is, or what he or she has in everyday life. Baptism anoints us into the sacramental priesthood of Jesus and he draws us into his offering which includes our own. One of the deepest convictions that has grown out of my thirty years as a priest is that Jesus wants everyone to share in his priesthood, to become so identified with him that we become Eucharist, sacrament, bread and wine for the world. The Holy Spirit is poured into us "to teach us to understand the gifts that he has given us" (1 Cor 2:12).

The Eucharist has its full effect and its full reality only in the hearts of the faithful when they live their priesthood in a life offered to the Father in Christ. Christ's presence in us activates our capacity to sense and awaken his presence in our neighbor. And when we give ourselves and receive another, Christ is rendered present in our midst.

We become a world church sharing the priesthood of Christ.

Every day I celebrate the Eucharist, and as I break the bread and pour the wine of life, I pray and dream that someday it will raise up prophets and evangelists and martyrs out of my people, beginning with myself. The Eucharist is the sacrament of martyrs and prophets and evangelists. Yet it is even more startling to realize that the Eucharist is the food of the "anawim," the poor, the little ones — children and elderly, retarded and handicapped, homeless nobodies.

He comes each day to the anonymous multitudes, to people as ordinary and undistinguished as sand on the beach, as grass in the field. No one is insignificant to him, no one is anonymous. He is always loving each one into being, always drawing them deeper into his heart. He grows flowers in the desert and dandelions in the middle of the freeways. He extravagantly gives life and beauty to every person, every thing, every place. He lets his sun and rain come down upon the worthy and the unworthy. He feeds the anonymous multitudes with bread from heaven, even in the middle of the desert.

And yet the reality of this marvelous gift is that he cannot come to us unless we go to him; he cannot give himself unless we give ourselves; he can only come to us through the gift we give to him. This is the great exchange! Our life, food, and drink offered to him becomes his gift to us. The priesthood of Christ, the sacrifice of Jesus, becomes the invitation to become priest of our own lives, to make the real offering of the sacrifice of oneself. "Do this in memory of me.... Be Eucharist." The more we receive his body and blood, the more we are drawn into his priesthood, into his abandonment. The more radically we hunger for him, the more radically he fills us.

And so, I wonder as I continue to hunger for him, as I abandon myself into his hands each day, what will he continue to dream for me? Will he teach me to love more, to lay down my life? O Lord, that I might see your presence in everyone, everything! *Now* is the great beginning.

Postscript

As for me, my life is already being poured away as a libation, and the time has come for me to be gone. I have fought the good fight to the end; I have run the race to the finish; I have kept the faith.

2 Timothy 4:6-7

I have so often asked people that question God asked Adam and Eve, "Where are you?" And now, as I move beyond my thirtieth year into the priest-hood, I ask the question of myself. Where am I? I still feel newly ordained. Everything still seems so new, so unlimited. And yet I am beginning to rec-ognize that time is accelerating and energy is wan-ing. I have had my first major surgery, I have been in danger of dying and have received the sacrament of the sick. I have had the first glimpses of the dis-tant shore of retirement and death. The wisdom of the ages is blunt. Reluctantly, I am compelled to acknowledge that I am no longer young; that I, too, am mortal; that there is a time limit. I move closer to those scanning the horizon for the Master's return.

Sometimes I envy my lay friends who are enjoying their "thirty and out" early retirement before the mid-fifties. But as I reached that marking, I found myself reflecting on the possibility of "thirty and in." I feel as though it has taken me thirty years to grow into Christ's priesthood. As I gather the fragments of my thirty years of priesthood, I cannot even begin to count the leftover baskets that are filled to overflowing. "His priesthood working in me has done infinitely more than I could have asked or imagined" (Eph 3:20).

I celebrated my thirtieth anniversary Eucharist on December 16, 1986. I had offered my first Mass at the Clementine Altar on the tomb of St. Peter in Rome. That chapel was so small that it seemed I would touch either wall as I stretched out my arms. There was hardly room for a dozen people. I had hoped to celebrate there again on my thirtieth, but it was under repairs. Instead I was asked to celebrate at the Altar of St. Peter's Chair, beneath the magnificent alabaster window of the Holy Spirit. I faced the papal altar and could see beyond into the vast open space of the main aisles of St. Peter's Basilica. In thirty years, my Eucharist had grown and expanded from an underground crypt to a window onto the world.

So much has changed in the priesthood but the one reality that cannot change is the Eucharist, the source and summit of each priest's life. The Eucharist can become so much a part of one's day that it becomes as natural and spontaneous, as much of a habit, as dinner or sleep. The Eucharist enters the blood stream, the heart beat, the rhythm of breathing.

The Eucharist never ceases to be a burning bush. It can become so intimate, so habitual and domesticated; yet like fire, it always remains dangerous, strange, shooting off a spark or a light that startles and wakens you. It is a well, the depths of which have never been fathomed, from which springs up water, turning to wine, changing into his blood and carried to the altar on high. It is Tabor where Jesus calls his disciples to bathe in his transfigured glory, a glory so transparent it is a wonder our faces do not have to be veiled!

Even after thirty years, or perhaps because of the thirty years, I remain in awe and wonder at the mystery of Jesus Eucharist. It has become more *kadosh,* more *hagios,* more *sanctus,* more holy. I continually find myself being drawn into something, Someone, so vast, so immense, so transcendent, so incomprehensible, so distant, so strange, so inexpressible, yet so intimate, so close, so tiny, so personal, so faithful, so inner, so quiet, so gentle, so silent that a whisper would sound like thunder.

Thirty years ago I had etched around the lip of my chalice the words in Latin, "I am the Vine, you are the branches, without me you can do nothing." Those words of John's gospel haunted me before I was ordained and now, thirty years into the priesthood, they continue to haunt me and, in some way, strangely console me. I have so often prayed, spoken and written about priesthood. The mystery of Christ's priesthood, as deep and vast as the ocean, washes the shores of every culture, every generation. What a small fragment of his priesthood becomes visible and transparent in any parish or diocese, any priest or bishop. The tide comes in and the tide goes out, and each day the shore of the continents are changed forever. The priesthood of Christ never changes, yet is always changing because of those he chooses, creating in them a desire to follow him and to stay with him.

Each priest makes a distinctive and significant difference, leaves some imprint, some deposit, a word, a breath of the body of Christ. My life seems to disappear so quickly into history, yet nothing is lost because it is part of the body of Christ and is lifted up into eternity day after day. What an incredible leap of faith for a priest to believe the words of Jesus, "You have not chosen me, I have chosen you!" Each priest must borrow the words of Jesus again and again. What Jesus says of his Father living in him, a priest must say of Jesus living in himself. "I do nothing of myself; it is Jesus living in me who is doing this." In Eucharist, in reconciliation, in baptisms, weddings and anointings, the living power at work is Jesus. Without him the priesthood is nothing and the priest is the greatest fool of all. As Paul proclaimed, "if Christ has not been raised then our preaching is useless and your believing it is useless; indeed we are shown up as witnesses who have committed perjury before God" (1 Cor 15:14-15).

Unique and solitary is the faith of a priest at the altar; but the Eucharist is never private; it is always communal and universal. A special community, a precious family, is created and generated in the Eucharist. The eucharistic family of a priest is a great gift. The faith-filled people who gather confirm his faith and energize him with the faith of centuries. The priest need not ask, "Who is my mother and my brothers and my sisters?" He knows them, he experiences them in the breaking of the bread, and his heart burns within him as he goes with them on their way. Together they do the will of their Father in heaven.

A priest is one who remembers and dreams, who renders present the past and the future. Eucharist is the sacrament of remembering what has gone before and of longing for what is yet to be. It hallows time and place and people. A priest's life is an unbroken journey from one Eucharist to another, from one sacramental time and place to another.

Once I foolishly said to a friend that all my dreams were fulfilled by the time I was thirty. She quietly responded, "I have not dreamed all of my dreams." That wisdom comes so often to me as I hold my chalice each day. The base of my chalice is made of a large piece of rock crystal, symbolic of the joyful mysteries of Jesus' early life. During my first year as a priest, the crystal base of the chalice developed a crack from top to bottom, yet somehow it did not split and separate. The crack became a mirror of my own fragility. I am cracked completely through, but God has held me together as faithfully as I have held to him as my life and light, grace and truth.

No matter what cathedrals are built, no matter how solid and unshakable they appear; we humans still live in the fragile tents of our body. I carry the faces, the words, the prayers, the wounds of the eucharistic communities I've celebrated with in my heart and they carry mine in theirs. No matter what achievements in culture or science, we will be nomads, wanderers, pilgrims on our journey to the stars. He has created the way, he has gone ahead and is waiting in the place he has prepared for us, yet, he comes daily to be with us on the journey.